woodnote

woodnote

Christine Deavel

Ch— Deavel

For the Rofkar Family — With gratitude and delight!

The Dorothy Brunsman Poetry Prize
BEAR STAR PRESS

Printed on acid-free paper in the United States of America.

10 9 8 7 6 5 4 3 2 1

Direct all inquiries to the publisher:
BEAR STAR PRESS
185 Hollow Oak Drive
Cohasset, CA 95973
530.891.0360 / www.bearstarpress.com

Cover art: *Exposure* by Jacqueline Barnett, courtesy of the Francine Seders Gallery, Seattle
Book and cover design: Beth Spencer
Author photograph: Natalie Fuller

Woodnote is set in Minion Pro and Myriad Pro.

Bear Star books are distributed by Small Press Distribution: www.spdbooks.org.

ISBN: 978-0-9793745-8-6
Library of Congress Control Number: 2011903192

The publisher would like to thank Dorothy Brunsman for her support of the press since its inception.

ACKNOWLEDGEMENTS

American Letters & Commentary: two sections of "Home Town (Over and Over)"
Fence: portions of "Woodnote"
Golden Handcuffs Review: "Economy"
Talisman: "Hidden" and a section of "Home Town (Over and Over)"

"Woodnote" and "Home Town (A Savior Saves by Not Saving)" appeared in the chapbook *Box of Little Spruce*, published by LitRag Press.

"Drawn" appeared in an earlier form as "Of the Bird's Wing, There are Tracts of Feathers" in *Looking Together: Writers on Art*, published by the Frye Art Museum / University of Washington Press.

TABLE OF CONTENTS

Acknowledgements

one

HIDDEN

Hidden
as a toy balloon in the sky is
and is not
As a hawk in the sky
over a pasture
is and is not
What is hidden
like what is beautiful
is in the eye
You may be a thing
stained with tinctures
and packeted in muslin
and tinkered up in a small balsa box
and set on a root-cellar shelf
But you are not hidden
unless someone seeks you
and does not know you are
a thing dyed by walnut shells
that has been wrapped
in a saved sheet of tinfoil
and folded into the pocket square
of a discarded apron
and closed inside a jumble drawer.

HOME TOWN (OVER AND OVER)

Dragonfly in hover,
you are not a ghost
over the river

and the river is
not a ribbon
of memory

unwinding below your pulse.

I am a ghost

over an earlier river.
I am a ribbon
of smoke over

a ribbon of filmstrip.
We are related
through hovering.

Where did you go on your walks?
   This was my town.
Whom did you see on your walks?
   No one. I remember no one.
Who saw you on your walks?
   Everyone saw me.
What did you see on your walks?
   A casement of bees on an abandoned house.
   The samples at the monument-maker's.
   Tree, tree, tree, tree, tree.
Why did you go on your walks?
   I was answering.

the maple   the walnut   the oak
I was ever unhurried   unhurrying   tired

when the glass in the window was warm
I lay down

when the glass in the window was cold
I stretched out

and outside the trees hung
green pictures for me

and outside the iced-over branches
dazzled me

so I rose and dressed
or undressed a bit and walked

about the town
slowly about the town

fetching nothing
but the end and back

the gyroscope that held my mind
made lying down and walking one

the gyroscope that held my heart
spun

I heard them
and the trees heard me

porch lights then
were not left on at night

"We are done
with visitors now

and the one who should be home
is"

How big was the town?
One crockery bowl filled with red leaves.

What was its density?
The weight of a bee on a bridal-wreath branch
times the sag of a clothesline.

What were your increments?
The beats of the luna-moth's wings and the pieces of coal
through the chute to the basement.

Who charted these things?
It's not too late to have noticed, it's not too late
to see.

I unroll like a bank of clouds
over the town

I darken it
with my massive self

as a little girl
in a dead-man's float

I see poorly without my glasses
and through the blue

but there's pleasure in looking
at color and shape

in pretending all the pebbles
belong to you

no rescuing needed
for town or for me

collar bones
shown because of the heat

a shirtless man
mowing
a woman in a print shift

looking for their
girl in the blue bathing suit
who was making a walk

to the four corners
of her living block
corralled

by the dusk
the bit of the heat
in her mouth

she was dumb
unable to answer
the naming mother

her response
was her return

caraway   caraway

storm windows
are not windows into
storms but away from them

what is winter
    it is a father on a ladder
    with glass

caraway   caraway

sauerkraut
potatoes

what is winter   mother
mother   what is winter

a bowl   a heavy bowl
                    filled

caraway   caraway

                daughter
                set the table

                what is winter
                daughter

I walk to school
    and the wind reddens me

I walk home
and the snow coddles me
forgetfully

caraway   caraway

not a spice for a girl to use
but she eats it
                mother
        she eats it
                father

this is winter

The starchy yarn of spring came
and knitted itself into a blue hyacinth
then unraveled that
and tatted itself into a columbine
then snipped it up
coated it in paste
and spread itself out to make a sky
but cut a small patch
to suggest a doorway
and gave the tiny remnant
to a little girl who
walked about the town below
opening and closing
the little blue door.

From a maple as thick as heat
took a leaf, a summer leaf,
and tore it to place
between front teeth and tongue
to make a new skin for the mouth,
to make an other green sound.
Took green through the eye
and into the hand
and into her mouth (o breath)
and announced.

Remind me,
what was our tithe?
  The peony flowers.
What were our jewels?
  The peony buds.
What was our relief?
  The peony shoots.
Who kept watch for us?
  The peony roots,
  set so shallow
  the cyes could nearly see.

The small white clover flower in my hand,
an implement or a lament.

The brown crisp leaf with the acorn cap,
a letter of longing or a warrant.

This clinker was shoveled, spent,
from the furnace,

but my dear ones, street lights
are flickering on inside my chest.

Seasonless evening sky
all-season evening sky
unable to locate
myself by looking

utterly empty of
cloud, plane, bird, or ghost
it cannot last
as it is lasting

palest blue long and wide
it cannot stay
as it is staying
cipher sky

or pure sky
or sky before or after an ending
looking at it is no use
for mooring

how can it hold
as it is holding
who am I
when I stand below it

pale invisible everything
palest full nothing

Do you know the mourning dove?
She began and closed the day.

What is her song?
Once there was a world, gone, gone.

Speak of the blue jay.
He was the grit
that polished the hot green shade.

And what of the cardinal?
O stop. That call is lost to me.

Open your book of snow and look.
Red, red ascending.

HOME TOWN (A SAVIOR SAVES BY NOT SAVING)

who might—to might—give out a kindness
to weakness, pay out a kindness

Through our covered bridge
Scatter-Love Abiding, come

over loose boards with slits of the river
Scatter-Love Abiding, come
with Your slow face
and Your empty hands

unshocked by August out the other side
sex of sky, nothing swollen like we

under the tree shimmer
and over popping tar

come

though
Smudged Glasses wants else than this
and Daylily Heart wants this and more
and who is hair-twirly sad and sour?
O gritty citizen longing

let kindness
that is Cold-Love Abiding
walk maple-nut scattered
unto the tattery edges of this town

out the bridge mouth
come unpuzzled this
Particle-Love Abiding

two

DRAWN

The bird's wing is made of tracts of feathers, each with its own name. The crown, the breast, the mantle. But also there are the coverts, those layers of feathers beneath, that cover the base of the feathers below. Covert means shelter, a place for the hidden. Before white settlement, Indiana was covered by more than two billion trees. Barely two centuries ago, it was nearly completely a canopy of forest. And threading the forest were millions of acres of marshes and swamps, almost a fourth of the state. By the Eel River, not far from the Wabash River, I grew up in a town surrounded by vast, flat tracts of farmland. I know there was a land of forest and marsh, and I know that it is gone. The knowledge may be a kind of covert, the absence become presence again, the gone become hidden. Knowledge not as comfort but as shelter.

PRIMARY COVERTS

Short-Eared Owl
A young man who was crossing
        a partially inundated field
    counted these birds as they arose
                        before him,
and at one time there were thirty in the air.
        There was only one tree
        and they all alighted
        on that tree.

Least Bittern
The nest,
a few inches to a foot above
                    the water,
    placed upon a few stems
        or leaves of the cat-tail,

which the bird
  had evidently bent down
                and arranged
    into a shallow, insecure nest.
Did not see the bird
on the nest in a single case,
so watchful and shy
are they.

King Rail
One nest, twelve eggs,
found by Mr. Steinman,
built in over-flowed meadow;
consisting of broken, dried cane;
the nest proper very small
and the eggs piled up
on top of each other.

Henslow's Sparrow
Hearing a rustle in the grass,
  looked down and saw a bird
                which ran like a mouse.
It stuck its head under some
                leaves and grass,
  leaving its tail exposed.
Had to back some distance to shoot it.
    The males were in full song.

Black-Crowned Night Heron
Large numbers in the heronry,
and many flying over
carrying sticks
and building.

White-Crowned Night Heron
The nests among the tall ash
and sweet gum trees
                in a creek bottom.
Several fine specimens
were secured, and it was noted that
        the delicate, almost luminous,
            yellowish buff of the forehead
                very soon faded.

Hypotheticals List
rare visitor   rare winter visitor   perhaps by mistake
now considered an error   accidental   mentioned by error
former resident   perhaps found in the lower valley   rare
this is an error   occasional in winter   straggler   it seems doubtful
known from but few localities   accidental northward
possibly may not be found at all within our limits

To move through land as a place of subsistence is different from moving through it as a place of commercial surplus. Between 1830 and 1840, Indian landholdings in Indiana decreased from nearly 4 million acres to 30,000. Eventually those, too, would be ceded or partitioned among the remaining members of the remaining tribe, the Miami of Indiana, no longer recognized by the United States government. I lived by Miami Avenue and belonged to the Tribal Trails Girl Scout Council. The town was giving itself hints. The words were retaining a place of subsistence.

GREATER COVERTS

The cessions are as follows:

A tract lying east of a line running opposite the mouth.
    Of a portion and finally of the remnant.
Small and great confluence bounded
                                by crimson.
    Woods, the breadth and in tracing.
    Of that river, strips, minutely laid down.
The December end of the portage place.
    Also the overlapping voice of all lakes.

The red-winged blackbird has a supple song, like falling water, a fitting thing since it is drawn to water. A red-winged blackbird perched on a fence at the edge of a ditch that edges a field is a sighting worth calling out in the car on a drive that is nearly all fields. The draining of great tracts of marshland in order to make of them great tracts of farmland was made possible by the ready availability of clay pipe, which lined the ditches and drained the water away. Toward the end of the 19th century, hundreds of factories in Ohio, Indiana, and Illinois made earthenware tile, as it is called, to carry the water away from the land. The red of the red-winged blackbird is the startling thing in the landscape, which is field upon field upon field. It is worth saying its name out loud.

LESSER COVERTS

Cracking pearlymussel (possibly extirpated) Fanshell Fat pocketbook
Northern riffleshell Orange-foot pimpleback (possibly extirpated)
Pink mucket pearlymussel Purple cat's paw pearlymussel Rayed bean
Ring pink mussel Sheepnose Tubercled-blossom (possibly extirpated)
White cat's paw pearlymussel White wartyback pearlymussel

MEDIAN COVERTS

How clear this space. Sore want to do,
a seed left dark or drowned.
Leafed fear, sewn pelt, a cut that flew.
Risk rest—whose voice is bound?

Low wings from trees, a love pure red.
Redress is nightly turned.
What listens for us, us of thread?
Snow word, a gate in earth.

Knowledge comes as a covering snow; below is the old understanding. And knowledge from learning, that is, from words, unlike through experience, gives no memory (except of the moment the blind was raised). But to walk through it, to walk through the snow as it falls, is to walk through another's memory, even if it is only the land's. There is the cardinal, unseen until now.

UNDERWING COVERTS

Following the courses thereof,

to the place of beginning,
to the place of beginning,
thence to the place of beginning.

SOURCES

Primary Coverts: Lines taken from *The Birds of Indiana: with Illustrations of Many of the Species, Prepared for the Indiana Horticultural Society and Originally Published in its Transactions for 1890* by Amos W. Butler (Wm. B. Burford, printer and binder, 1892). These birds are endangered in Indiana.

Greater Coverts: Words and phrases drawn from *Cessions of Land by Indian Tribes to the United States: Illustrated by Those in the State of Indiana* by C.C. Royce (Washington DC: Government Printing Office, 1881).

Lesser Coverts: Drawn from *Endangered, Threatened, Proposed, and Candidate Species* (U.S. Fish and Wildlife Service, Region 3: Illinois, Indiana, Iowa, Michigan, Minnesota, Missouri, Ohio, Wisconsin, February 2007).

Median Coverts: A sonic translation of the poem "No Bird" by Theodore Roethke.

Underwing Coverts: Drawn from descriptions of land ceded by the Miami Nation of Indiana in the treaties of 1818 and 1834.

three

PIECE BY PIECE

In a thunderstorm
do not talk on the telephone.

The lightning will find you
talking

to someone not here.

Listen
you better listen

to what's happening

over your own house.

It is possible to
believe in the chrysanthemum
To follow its will
for it has none
Come unhumbly
and lower yourself
to be drawn into the straw
of its fragrance
peeled by a button of yellow
out of your days

Even as you are chinked
into your blankets
and pricked with radio light
it is possible
to know the chrysanthemum
glows under the window
sips the dark
not for you
but catches you all the same

≈

A spirit searched the shrubs,
sometimes all of them at once,
and rose up and shook the trees
and then shoved the clouds.
At first it had just flicked
one daylily leaf over and over.
It must have been thinking
and stretched out in the grass.
Then it sat up and swatted
the lilac. When it stood
it hit its head on the chimes,
which must have aroused it,
because it began rummaging
and scraping and grasping
and flinging, and I think
it was humming in an exasperated way,
a growling, puffy hum before a sentence.
Such as, *Push your hair out of your eyes,*
you whippery, leafy, dangling things,
meaning you and your viburnums.

~

What the bat wrote
on the evening sky
I can't say.

What did bat write
on evening's sky?
Cannot say.

Bat wrote
on evening's sky.
Please say.

~

Dark doctor's office once
turned from a house on Main Street
blinds drawn
light from a glass-shaded little lamp
dark leather armchair
dark leather couch
dark cigarette air
intricate pedestal ashtray
marble and brass
seal and imprimatur
like the diploma
a wrought-iron shadow over his desk
He in the dark
I in the dark
Mother in the dark
all of us gentle
all of us careful
Outside
the town was bright day
the day was sharp town
We sat in our trembling triangle
as light kept welling
through a thick black cord.

~

In the neighborhood of the flaked-to-cloudy houses and the akimbo stairs.

    I remember someone's knuckled-under fence.

    Someone's thought of a flower garden tried to articulate itself each year.

And in one second there was a German Shepherd mouth in a volley. Hers was

    an unwondered-at brain. I wonder now. Terror she left uncompleted.

Here is a viewing globe for shaking. Sycamore and maple in full swell.

    A stepladder's worth of streets with no sidewalks. Light that comes

    in narrow troughs. Unpeopled but I a person and the dog a being.

    I a being and the dog a person of interest in the terror.

    I a person of interest in her terror.

    ~

The walnut is a dangerous beauty.
The nuts in their green cases
fall and strike sometimes,
less predictable than bees.
Best to leave the yard mostly
to it for awhile.
And the darkening, softening casings
stain the hands and the feet of the one
languidly putting them in a pail.
Straight as light, unmarred,
rivulet-perfect brown bark
on a trunk that is worth something
because a man knocked at the door
to buy it (that is, cut it down).
The walnut is a messy tree,
Mother said with no pleasure.
But she left it where it is.

~

Quercus (the oak) for staring

Acer (the maple) for stairs

the elevation of the county
is in the trees

easier to climb a mountain
than rest in the tips of a sweet gum

≈

When the warning siren stops
have an ambulatory song

In a leafy fury
    spin the rakings of you up
    into a tree
So, be a bird

Quillous, beak-sure,
hooked feathers in a color
the color of a color

Tell!   "Bird-be-here!
        Bird-be-here!"
Till comes, as must,
again, wind
and all you all
make, sudden, a flock.

                ∼

BUTTON BOX

Pop the stone out of its setting
and suck on it, suck on it
Now you are the sea

This pile of swept up sticks
would make a fine nest
for someone I don't know

The robin carries my bliss in her basket

Don't anthropomorphize me!
Let me be the tree that I am

With the gears of this block
walking makes the corner dog bark

When we speak bird
it's pidgin

Longing
L'empty
Levitate

Where is your mother
buried? Then, under earth. Now,
under earth and snow.

Longer nights. I want
to wear her sweater. But to
wash it. What sorrow!

Blackberry
    Storm
    at the end
    of a twig

Yew needles
    Who wept these?

Sycamore leaf
    I hear it walking down the stairs

four

WOODNOTE

Song the First

I must leave the door open
in case she wants to come see me.

I leave the door open
should she want to find me.

If I kept it closed
the wooden door would be
      a vertical pond
she would float along

she a slow vapor would float along

      What is standing up or lying down
      to her? The body suffers each
      the same.

      But I believe she is not suffering.

      She is just intimately parallel
      to floor or roof or lawn or shop window
      or my body. She is hydrophilic,
      lithophilic, sanguiphilic, spiraphilic,
      ossophilic, terraphilic, lignaphilic,

her body as if it were a mass of
charged metal filings.

She is near but cannot enter again.

A Whispering

In the corner of the room there is a gesture.

Just a gesture. In every room, in the right-most corner.

From the right-most corner of my eye, in the living room
        or bathroom, bedroom, hallway, I see her-gesture.

Just the gesture of the arm in the navy long-sleeved dress
        (just the sleeve, cuffed, buttoned in mother-of-pearl).

The hand will rise or swing out for . . .
                                    or fall.

In all the rooms I enter. As I enter, there is her-gesture,
in the right-most corner. Even after I've settled and napped
or read or talked long about an ill.

She is by her ornamental table, her hip at the carved edge.

In every room in the right-most corner is the round wood table
and her hip at its edge.

Just the arm and the hip.

Just the gesture.

Just the table, the arm, and the hip.

And the gesture
like breath, like breathing.

A Story

The wood of the clock is an atomizer.

On the mantel was the graceful hillock of clock.

   The ring of numbers   behind the lens
         is a wake in a still pond,
   the drop of the stone when time started.

O the wood of the clock is an atomizer and in it

            is

           her distillation.

Path to you through the glass-filled doors first the front door
dark wood frame then the glassed-in porch door dark wood frame
then step up just a sigh-step up to the living room It's me hello

       One door unlocked   The next door unlocked

    UP you were UP the sharp slant of carpeted stairs

      washing your hands in the large, empty bathroom,
the crisp, somnambulent bathroom. Nearby were

                        the comb
                        the boar-bristle brush
                        the small, round mirror
all made of wood. Each one a lovely hand.

OR in the front bedroom or the back bedroom

(both diaphanously empty with bed and
3 to 5 boxes and a piece of art)
you were
putting things away
away   away.

OR in your own bedroom, at the round-shouldered dressing table,

on its little exclamation of bench, closing

one of the hand's-width drawers running down

on either side of you

closing a drawer mouth because you have just set the little packet
back in its cheek.

Hello?   Because the wood of the clock
is   an
atomizer.

I stood in the living room.

It's me!

I stood in the wash of the clock.

I'll be down. I'll be right down.

Hymn

      The fingernails are the portals.

The fingernails the eyes,
the fingernails the wood
               revealed.

The fingernail will show the grain.

The fingernails   the true wood
                     revealed.

The ridged thumbnail was coated with clear polish

as if it were   a little table

    a lovely rosewood table

        where the grain
          has been revealed.

        Not for sitting at
        and sometimes for placement
            but
        for the grain revealed

    primarily that:

Here was the true wood revealed.

A Story

Where there was hardship

        between the mother and the mother's mother

there was the collection
of pitchers, also
      that they both might stand and admire,
      or touch and turn,

       in their dresses
           next to each other

  and the eyes, the moist eyes,

      watched the beauty of the pitchers
        on the dark wood ledge
        that ran along the windows.

   Afternoon of light through the swirled or pebbled glass
made viscous with color.

The watching of the pitchers:

      a song.

      They sang together
      the watching of the pitchers.

Sweet lyric, sweet round, sweet lyric, sweet round.

Song the Second

The wooden gloves and the hat of wood, too.

The wooden camisole and half-slip:

          these in the old oiled dresser.

In the shadowy end of the cedar-lined closet:

    the beautiful   gleaming

        wood dress.

Who waited once, and who is waiting now,
              to wear them.

Once, they say, there was a wooden purse
and in it a little wood book
and a whole ring of wooden keys.

True or not,

     among us all each
          felt the loss,
     among us all each
          feels the loss.

One Ditty

At some point,   perhaps,   there should not be
        water
          on the wood.

Just because there is only water
          with a bit of garlic
            and ginger
steeping
      there is soup.

But at some point perhaps, when the wood

     has been transformed,
and it is in the home, water should be
           kept   from   it.

       Ho ho! The wooden spoon!

              What a lovely twist or joke or divinity!

In the soup pot, the wood is a tree again

          and finds its water,
      and its little bit
       of sustenance
from the garlic and ginger.

O the wooden spoon is a tree again

and
    who can keep from crying.

Song the Third, Parts One and Two

1.

The March twig is a skein of woodiness
barely wood.

What is that then?

The snag that tipped in the backyard was
an old, ill-planted *Cornus florida*.

That was wood, once.   Or still?

Neither of those would make a table.
Spindly or rotten.

Oh?   Oh?

Woven whips, yes?
Or glue-bound, soft-as-soap pieces?

Well, all inventions are possible.
But those are not the small carved table
                in the corner.

The table waited and then arrested.
The table is made of wood that thickened,
then stopped.

But rot is still possible.

True.
That table is everything.

And there is still wind in it, wind
in its branches.

Yes, it makes me chill.

2.

The rivers in the wood flow from the table.
The rivers have been daylighted there.
The water slips from another world

                              (the ever-dark forest
                              the cloud-understanding
                              the time-start)

and slips back in there.

I am moved at the river revealed.
I am stuttered with fear.
I am humbled and so made joyous.

I am wondering, darling,
I am wondering, love, is there entering the river
                                        here?

five

ECONOMY

:: A cloudy day :: A cloud day :: A snowy morning :: Thawing ::
A frost morning :: A pleasant day :: A thawy day :: A misty day ::

After the writer of the diaries passed away
the diaries played as a loop
The first day as alive as any in them

:: 8 above zero :: A misty afternoon :: A nice day :: A nice day ::
A mild day :: A snowy afternoon :: A gloomy day :: A cold wind ::

The rows of volumes stood up
and opened themselves to the eternal
June 23, 1914, is a picture on the wall
If everyone there is dead then that is living
Only we the alive are truly dead
Dead to all (to the so much vaster)
but the present

:: A stormy day :: Snows some :: A rainy day :: A rainy forenoon ::
A nice day :: A dreadful wind :: A damp morning :: Rained a little ::

ink was sipped onto the page
ink is sapped from the narrow page
reading is reedy

:: A hot day :: A warm day :: A heavy rain ::

I am slipping
through her rushes

    I have ended up with a set of diaries from a distant relative. I say ended up as if
something were complete now and settled. My father, who had them before and had
his packaging store send them to me, is a closer relative and knew her, the writer of the
diaries. He thinks the situation is settled now and that the diaries are in their proper place.
The story is complete. The road has ended here.
    A road may be used to go two ways. I had not planned on travel.
    Sarah's diaries cover over 50 years. She lived her entire life in rural northern Indiana,
not far from where I was born. I am resisting being precise. No, that's not exactly what I
mean. I am resisting the fencing in by numbers and names and something more. I would
say facts, but then I think you'll resist believing me. I would like us both to stand in the
same place.

:: We sew :: We wash :: We did Saturday work :: We finished quilt ::
We bake bread :: We washed :: We cleaned upstairs :: We washed
and sewed :: We made molasses :: We finished ironing :: We work
at cherries :: We ironed and scrubbed :: We dry corn :: We dry corn ::
We wash start coal fire & wrap sweet potatoes :: we sew ::

I would like to study the day's lesson from the Book of Sarah,
who hath done what she could.
I am reading each of her days for a double score and more,
and I know her not.
I am untutored and reading the text of Sarah.

:: We washed & canned 15 quart pickles :: We set strawberry plants ::
We work at Mary's red skirt :: We butcher 3 hogs for us 1 for Maggie ::

I read her days
yet she knows me not.
These are my texts:
The Poems of Emily Dickinson, The Granite Pail by Lorine Niedecker, Harriet the Spy
by Louise Fitzhugh, tattery collections of Chinese and Japanese haiku, collections of
Doonesbury comic strips, of Mutts comic strips, of Peanuts comic strips, The Ether Dome
by Allen Grossman, Poems of Paul Celan, Anne Carson's Glass, Irony and God.

Her people were my people.
She gave my father $5 when he graduated from high school.
Her text is not my text.
How can her text be my text?
I am the keeper of her text.

Now there is a terribly hard rain.
I have written that down by the date,
October 5, 2004.
You can read me here, can't you.

:: Maggie & I go to see Aunt Ella :: Alma Ma & I to Mrs McClellan's ::
Pa & I to South Bend :: Pa Blanch & I to Walkerton :: Mary & I to Liberty ::
Mrs McClellan & I to Alma :: Alma & I to see Mable Anderson :: Pa & I
to John Baughman's sale :: Pa & I to Liberty :: Pa & I out to Dr Maranda ::
Mary John Floyd Maggie & I to South Bend :: Pa Alma & I to Leb Peffly
funeral age 67 :: Pa & I to church with Charly :: Maggie & I over to Alma
this afternoon ::

movement and no noise
noise without movement
                or even view of the maker
fully here because partially apprehended

enough is just enough
        to make you raise your head
     or to scratch into the brain her name
words and no body and no land
        nor any accumulation or scent
she like a cardinal
     sparked from a tree
they like a rain or a dusk or a gust
I see something move on this page
I know they are there

They walk along the holy page
They walk the holy page   the field
The fields lay out the boundary
of the days   the holy fields
the holy days that are all days

:: John helped Arthur haul a load of hay :: Pa help Charly this afternoon ::
Pa help Charly plant peppermint :: Pa help Arthur fix cement post :: Alma
help Maggie pack :: Mary help Edna :: Edna help Alma :: Arthur help
John plow corn :: Arthur help Mr Anderson thrash this afternoon ::
Ma help husk corn ::

keeping
    keeping to
  the edge
    the text   keeping the text
safekeeping the book

The Keeper, I am
not very good at it. Out there,

there are three full shrubs I let go, let go wild, walked from,
and under them is another, a fourth, an azalea I planted and loved.
Oh the three shrubs can go wild awhile, I was thinking,
but under is the forgotten azalea, covered, unblooming.
I look out the window and remember it now.

ache of stitches
            chest trussed up over the untrustworthy heart

:: Boy make hay :: Boy make hay :: Boy eat dinner at John supper
at Arthurs :: The boy put up sale bills for Arthur :: The boy planting
corn :: The boy finish corn :: Boy trying to cut wheat ::

might there be a curatorial cure
    i.e., you save
                to remedy others' ills
or is
        you keep to be kept
            watch to know watching
stroke the cat to feel
first the cat and then your hand

:: I paint tin roof :: I clean Ma bed room :: I sew :: I bake bread ::
I white wash in the cellar :: I clean isinglass to coal stove :: I clean
dining room this forenoon :: I work at cushion :: I dig potatoes
a part of the day :: I do Saturday work :: I can tomatoes :: I can
12 quart peaches :: I can 9 quart cherries :: I make 24 cups
elderberry jelly :: I made 9 cups grape jelly :: I sew ::

I'm just flailing
            —but that's how grain is removed

Is this a project?
What are you building?
Why are you building it?
Why build.

    In my dream, a young man had used what he could to create a block for printing, that is, he had used his forearm. He had carved into his own arm a border surrounding an ornament. He hath done what he could. His desire to print was profound. There was no pain in this dream. There was only the recognition of want moving someone to—what?—to foolishness, folly, iconoclasm, crudeness. In the room of the dream it was not the art he might make that mattered. The arm was inked and ready, but there was no paper near. In the room of the dream it was the exposure of desire. Desire to make. To make art. I squirm to write this. For two days I have been avoiding these words. He was foolish, a foolish village boy. But there was his wanting and his action. And they crowned him. How he seemed a sun coming through clouds. I turned and touched him where he was not carved. He hath done what he could with what he had where he was. Perhaps this is not desire. It may be this is trying to live. This is survival made visible. I am confused about desire and choosing to live. I am confused about art and the making of it. Is it better to make the mediocre because it allows you to get up every day? Or is it better to stop. You carve yourself to make and it's wrong. A mark of the naïve. But it nips at me. It is the mark of the true, it is the mark of love. It wasn't desire I saw. It was love, and I desired that.

:: Mr Wesleyan Rupel buried age 82 years :: Mrs Ruff died this evening :: Ralf infant son of Ed Hoffmans died age 12 hours :: Lillie Hostetter died this forenoon :: Lawrence Hostetters wife Lillie was buried this afternoon age 87 years :: Kate Steele died age 48 years 10 months :: Mr John Olinger died apoplexy :: Mrs Quigley died tonight at 2 o'clock :: Ray Cripe a boy :: Clide Keck a boy :: Edna Geyer a boy :: Henry Stull a boy :: Frank Fetzer a girl :: Ruth Heimes a girl :: Lydia Kelver a boy :: Emma Moon a girl :: Maud Vanscoik & DA Pearse married :: Russel Clark & Vera Naragon married :: George Anderson & Mable Schrader married :: Howard Smith & Miss Handretty married :: Iva Hardman & Russel Fair married :: Harry Clark & Blanch Bickle married ::

She, because she wrote it down
(though the ink is oxidizing into nothing
and I have no children)
For now she and I are together
She no children either
But she wrote them down
                              the days
So I turn toward her
who was turned toward me
Because she wrote out a bit of the day
she is the day
she makes the day
She is the source
I cannot say whether she is a creek
          spare and continuous
Or she is an ocean enduring
                              and monolithic
But we stood up out of Indiana fields
so creek she shall be ever and a day
until the ink has faded
How does fading go?
When they grade a creek
might it burl again elsewhere?
Does it raise a knot of waters
in the shush of the heart?
A swirl slipping to the eyes
and the woody old feet?

:: Jersey cow fresh :: Little red fresh :: Large red fresh :: Little jersey fresh ::

It would be a brave thing to spin the wingnuts on ghosts.
It is a brave thing to be slow enough to be a spinner of wingnuts on ghosts.
Courage, all. To touch the small chrome bodies of our dead ones.
The kit of the afterlife, for humans, trees, all animals, rocks, water,
a billion billion waves, flowers, clouds, all clovers, each flake of snow.
Wingnuts are made for fingers, not tools.
Come help assemble the afterlife in the current life. Courage, all.
In the afterlife, they bring their pieces to the living
to explain "whole."

:: Ma & Mary wash :: Ma & Maggie iron then work at hood :: Ma & Alma put in
quilt :: Ma & Maggie wash :: Ma & Prudence up to Mary this afternoon ::
Ma & Alma pick blackberries at McClellans can 4 quarts :: Ma & Alma to
see Vernon Steel he is complaining :: Ma & Mary put corn to dry ::

"Precious," he said, and meant it derisively. I understand and have said it myself. But I'm
sorry, sorry. Because now I'm thinking "cherished" and how close, how close to
"precarious."

:: Pa put up ashes :: Pa sell jersey calf :: Pa sows clover seed :: Pa burnt
the brush in peach orchard :: Pa hoed Arthur potatoes this forenoon ::
Pa shingle the shed over the barn tank :: Pa plow for Charly :: Pa top corn ::
Pa goes to Blissville to communion :: Pa trimmed up trees & fixed fence ::
Pa not well :: Pa not well :: Pa not well :: Pa thaws pump ::

Attached to the first page of the diary for 1952 is a bright red rectangle with perforated
sheets. At the top is written, "Place these strips inside your diary at once, on the day
PRECEDING the day you wish to remember." Below are five sentences, separated by
rows of dashes:
Tomorrow is your wife's birthday
Tomorrow is your husband's birthday

Tomorrow is your wedding anniversary
Tomorrow is your mother's birthday
Tomorrow is your father's birthday
Sarah never married. By midyear 1931, both her parents were dead.

:: Amos Peters did the preaching :: Brother Kesler preached :: Lafayette
did the speaking :: Pa did the speaking :: Brother Isenour preached ::
Brother Harly preached :: Pa did the talking :: Lafayette preached :: Sermon
preached by Brother Hoff of Chicago :: Lafayette preached ::

stiff zinnia   scratchy zinnia
serious Hoosier flower
most self-effacing loud color
an Anabaptist flower
when you are of age
you can choose
to be a zinnia

:: I clean up the sitting room & corn husk :: I did not feel good :: I did not feel
good :: Alma made my bonnet :: I feel bad :: I feel bad :: My face badly swollen ::
I feel a little better :: Pa Dortha & I keep house :: Pa & I planted melon & sweet
corn :: My face is bothering me :: I bake bread :: I not feeling good :: Alma
helps me with summer dress :: I help Alma with her cherries :: My face troubling
me :: Dr Maranda call in to see my face :: Alma does my washing ::

For a time I lost the ability or will to make linebreaks other than those that must come with
the edge of the page. I was walking a field from road to road, row after row.

:: John disk :: John thrash :: John plow :: John sow wheat :: John husk corn ::
John butcher ::

It is frightening to write and saddening not to. It has taken me three days to write that down; I have been thinking it for three days. Taken me. It has taken me. Three days it has taken me. What has taken me?

Last night I saw a performance by Jessica Williams, a jazz pianist, along with a bassist and drummer. Jessica Williams is tall and slender, her hair is straight and blonde-white, her voice when she speaks is a rustling—she looks like a sheaf of wheat. Her hands are large and subtle and fine, and with her brain (which must be the same) she assembled songs I know using a method of engineering that involves precipices, sluices, and pools. She and the bassist and the drummer kept rinsing me with dipper water. They kept floating me boxes that I opened and became happy. Toward the end of the evening she said to us, We've played some good music tonight—been played by it. That's not ego, she said, It's a reason to be on this earth for more than breathing.

It is tempting to write that Sarah's 54 years—nearly 54 years—of diaries, her purchase and filling (almost) of 54 diaries was a way for her to do more than breathe. Perhaps it is not temptation but hunger. I am nibbling at her rows of books. Pieces come off in my hands. I am rummaging, ruffling, sniffing, pawing. I am the dusk rat set on my search, my hunt, my errand, my thoughtless task. I am looking to undo my hunger. To do more than breathe.

O not to feed my hunger but to undo it.

She fed herself every day (I can barely put my hands on the typewriter keys to write this; I am winching myself here). She fed her day to the book—and then the book to herself? Did she read them after writing them, the days, the books? Why? She fed herself to her day, her day to her book, her book to herself whether she read it again or not. It is tempting —it is my hunger—to say she fed her hunger to do more than breathe on this earth by keeping her diaries. Now I am keeper of her diaries. Why is not to be a question for either of us any longer (I would like). Why is the face of worthwhileness. Why do it, asks the hunger, is the hunger. I open my mouth to the sun. Let us feed elsewhere.

:: A gloomy day :: A delightful day :: A heavy frost but nice day ::
A pleasant day :: A misty day :: A snowing day :: A little warmer ::

I shall live in the field of my sweater
for a time now.
I shall walk the field of my beige sweater
for a while.
A hard text tells me
not to seek comfort ever
for that is not how the soul
is shaped to fruition.
Or is that the easy text?
The true hard text says
be not suspicious of peace.
Come, holies,
make peace be
a comfort to me.

:: We washed and worked at pillow slips :: We clean yard :: We clean
parlor & parlor bed room :: We bake bread & clean up :: We clean
yard down at Mary's :: We done Saturday work ::

The obvious differences
and the obvious similarities
are not wherein the ardor
and so the story
lie. Like
and unlike in the gross-pattern,
align/misalign in the silhouette
are easy. No, that's not the thing
to be wary of—ease.
It is the dismissal hidden
in the ready assessment.

She is a sky with no stars.
I am a sky with no stars.
I cannot untangle myself
           from the grassblades.
But she walks through, walks through
  with her basket.
What happened, she wrote.
What happened, I wrote.
Read this, I asked.
And she?
We seeketh to make a straight line
in multitudinous ways.

:: Dortha & I keep house :: I send a box to Minnie bake bread churn &
bake cookie :: Alma & I fry down sausage this forenoon She goes to
Walkerton I finish it :: Pa & I pick apples this afternoon ::

It's a crinkly, chuffy, tipping body this.
It's a sharpened thing, picked,
pecked, moled up, come a lollipop
of a muffled and unmuffled thrum.
But what's amazing is
it's been completely broken,
smashed unto a mess of beach
then swept and tweezered back together,
glue-riddled, spackle-mangled, plaster-laced
together with itself as it was.
What a gingerbread village.
It's a papier-mâché globe over a popped balloon.
It's the holy mother popped from her mold.
I've already decided it's broken

and rebuilt everyday. I've already decided
it's fragile and rebuildable, it's razable
and erectable. I've already
refused any other ending.

:: John hauls manure :: John haul wood :: John haul manure & wood ::
John haul wood this afternoon :: John hauled logs :: John hauled
post this afternoon :: John hauled a load of poles :: John hauls manure ::
John hauls load of hay :: John hauled a load of hay :: John hauled
wood from the woods :: John haul out manure ::

Frightening
to wake up to
or with
the face of a violet.
But I may be ready.

:: I painted tank :: I wash & worked at dress :: I cleaned cupboard :: I
trimmed grapes :: I boil down sap :: I stamp a pair of pillow
slips :: I work at silk shirt :: I work at silk shirt :: I work at
silk shirt :: I washed & worked at cherries :: I scrub   clean
chicken & clean cellar :: I make me a gingham dress ::

The automobile has not been kind to my father's side of the family, and that is the side
that, if you knew them and me, would seem to be the side I am standing on. They
embraced the automobile early and early it turned and bit them, with the taking of Millard,
Charly and Alma's son, weeks after the accident, from infection. The doctors held counsel
and the family bought cloths to cool him, but he died at home, and Alma, Sarah's sister,
stopped her diary forever. I did not tell you that my father gave me Alma's diaries, too.
Charly would die, as well, in 1958, in an accident in a car he was driving. I was born that
year. Some years later, when I was still a child, my uncle's wife and two little girls, that is,

my aunt and two of my cousins, were killed by a drunk driver. My uncle was in the car, too, the only survivor of that family. When I was 15 my boyfriend lived 15 miles from me, so we rode back and forth on country roads between our houses in his car. One night a man with cataracts covering his eyes pulled onto the highway and hit us broadside on the passenger side, on my side, though I was sitting next to my boyfriend. I said, he's not going to stop, and he didn't. We all lived, me with stitches and a piece of glass removed from my face that I kept in a jewelry box. I wasn't keeping a diary then. I've never written about the wreck. I am writing about it now, in a brief way. I am not telling you a lot of the details. Later, after my boyfriend and I married and divorced, I married a man who, when he was 20, was hit by a car and severely injured. He was not driving the car, nor was he a passenger in it. He was outside a car to which he had no relationship until suddenly he had one forever. He is not nearly as afraid of cars as I am, as he should be, I would say, but I'm not sure that's true. I don't know what appropriate fear is. I did not tell you something about the carwreck that killed Charly, Alma's husband. I have delayed telling you. I knew I would tell you. It was a large fact, a big part of the story to me. I was saving it, for what I think is its proper place. I needed to move chronologically for a while, but now I am moving another way, like a pool of water. Sarah died in the car that day, too. Alma, who had stopped keeping a diary after her son died, wrote the last page in Sarah's diary. I think I am no longer writing about cars. I would like that.

:: First mess of peas ::

That is a green joy
Could write it down
for more than just a jot of the day
One round sweet green
green sweet round one
and one and one
have filled the bowl
Eat spoons of them
and write this down

Sometimes it's hard to remember who is alive and who is dead. And what is someone whom you've met only through a book, dead or alive?

:: First watermelon :: First pears :: First potatoes ::

Hold them and see how new you are

:: A rainy eve ::

She is quiet and
I am quiet
"I tinker around," she wrote
Not so broken that it's worth
paying someone

:: Monday August 10, 1914
    A good rain
    this afternoon
    Ma & I washed
    Pa hauled coal
    3 ton 160 pound
    John plowed
    Arthur painted
    summer kitchen ::

The robin singing
into the dusk
is not defining anything.
But I am still
grateful.

coda

Love Song

The door of the page is open for you.

And the end of each page is loneliness.

I crank in a new page to be near you.

I see the page with my sternum,

the wooden spoon at rest

on the small stove of my chest.

The still, wooden eye of my chest

watches the doorway.

The page is the doorway.

        Threshold

over which

wood calls out to wood.

In my heart

Charlotte Schütz Deavel
R. Gary Deavel
J.W. Marshall

ABOUT THE AUTHOR

Christine Deavel was raised in North Manchester, Indiana, and graduated from Indiana University and the University of Iowa. She is co-owner of Open Books: A Poem Emporium and lives in Seattle, Washington.